THE MOON BEFORE MORNING

Also by W.S. Merwin

Houses and Travellers
The Miner's Pale Children

TRANSLATIONS
Sun at Midnight (Poems and Letters by Musō Soseki)
(with Sōiku Shigematsu)
Collected Haiku of Yosa Buson (with Takako Lento)
Selected Translations 1948–2011
Sir Gawain & the Green Knight
Purgatorio
East Window: The Asian Translations
Pieces of Shadow: Selected Poems of Jaime Sabines
Vertical Poetry (Poems by Roberto Juarroz)
From the Spanish Morning
Four French Plays
Selected Translations 1968–1978
Euripedes' Iphigeneia at Aulis
(with George E. Dimock Jr.)
Osip Mandelstam: Selected Poems
(with Clarence Brown)
Asian Figures
Transparence of the World (Poems by Jean Follain)
Voices (Poems by Antonio Porchia)
Products of the Perfected Civilization
(Selected Writings of Chamfort)
Twenty Love Poems and a Song of Despair
(Poems by Pablo Neruda)
Selected Translations 1948–1968
The Song of Roland
Lazarillo de Tormes
Spanish Ballads
The Satires of Persius
Poem of the Cid

ANTHOLOGY
Lament for the Makers: A Memorial Anthology

W.S. Merwin

THE MOON BEFORE MORNING

Copper Canyon Press

Port Townsend, Washington

Cover art: Daniel Sullivan, *Haiku Moon* (www.danielsullivanphotography.com)

Copper Canyon Press is in residence at Fort Worden State Park in Port Townsend, Washington, under the auspices of Centrum. Centrum is a gathering place for artists and creative thinkers from around the world, students of all ages and backgrounds, and audiences seeking extraordinary cultural enrichment.

LIBRARY OF CONGRESS CATALOGING-IN-PUBLICATION DATA

Merwin, W. S. (William Stanley), 1927–

[Poems. Selections]

The moon before morning.

pages cm.

Includes bibliographical references.

ISBN 978-1-55659-453-3

1. Title.

PS3563.E75A6 2014

811'.54—dc23

2013031662

35798642

FIRST PRINTING

COPPER CANYON PRESS

Post Office Box 271

Port Townsend, Washington 98368

www.coppercanyonpress.org

For Paula

ACKNOWLEDGMENTS

I wish to thank the editors of the following publications, in which these poems first appeared.

The American Poetry Review: "Beginners," "Coming of Age," "Dew Light," "Garden Music," "The Green Fence," "Looking Up in the Garden," "One Summer," "The River One Summer Day," "A Step at a Time," and "Variation on a Theme"

The Kenyon Review: "Before Midsummer above the River," "By the Front Door," "From the Gray Legends," and "Homecoming"

The New York Review of Books: "Convenience," "Telephone Ringing," and "Urticophilia"

The New Yorker: "Alba," "A Breeze at Noon," "The Chain to Her Leg," "Forgotten Fountain," "Lear's Wife," "A Message to Po Chu-I," "Neither Here nor There," "The New Song," "Turning," and "Young Man Picking Flowers"

Poetry: "Identity"

CONTENTS

THE MOON BEFORE MORNING

I

HOMECOMING

Once only when the summer
was nearly over and my own
hair had been white as the day's clouds
for more years than I was counting
I looked across the garden at evening
Paula was still weeding around
flowers that open after dark
and I looked up to the clear sky
and saw the new moon and at that
moment from behind me a band
of dark birds and then another
after it flying in silence
long curving wings hardly moving
the plovers just in from the sea
and the flight clear from Alaska
half their weight gone to get them home
but home now arriving without
a sound as it rose to meet them

BY THE FRONT DOOR

Rain through the morning
and in the long pool a toad singing
happiness old as water

DEW LIGHT

Now in the blessed days of more and less
when the news about time is that each day
there is less of it I know none of that
as I walk out through the early garden
only the day and I are here with no
before or after and the dew looks up
without a number or a present age

THEFT OF MORNING

Early morning in cloud light
to the sound of the last
of the rain at daybreak dripping
from the tips of the fronds
into the summer day
I watch palm flowers open
pink coral in midair
among pleated cloud-green fans
as I sit for a while after breakfast
reading a few pages
with a shadowing sense
that I am stealing the moment
from something else
that I ought to be doing
so the pleasure of stealing is part of it

YOUNG MAN PICKING FLOWERS

All at once he is no longer
young with his handful of flowers
in the bright morning their fragrance
rising from them as though they were
still on the stalk where they opened
only this morning to the light
in which somewhere unseen the thrush
goes on singing its perfect song
into the day of the flowers
and while he stands there holding them
the cool dew runs from them onto
his hand at this hour of their lives
is it the hand of the young man
who found them only this morning

WHITE-EYE

In the first daylight one slender frond trembles
and without seeing you I know you are there
small foreigner to any word for you
no more foreign than I am in my own words
not making a sound now to call or answer
without hearing your voice I know who you are
there she comes now like a shadow in a whir of wings
before there are shadows and she calls in flight
one note and you answer with its other side
the long frond trembles again and you are gone
together with that one note between you
in a language I remember but do not know

FROM THE GRAY LEGENDS

Arachne wove the gray before daylight

from beyond the screen of fronds
before the birds before words
before the first stories
before voices

before Minerva's eyes were made
of that same gray

Arachne had her own beauty
seen or unseen
and she was older
she was already who she was

then it was day
and Minerva wove into daylight
from daylight
and she knew where the threads
were going in their stories
some of them
some of the time
and she claimed that she always knew

Arachne claimed nothing

Arachne did not have to know
she could wait
even when she was forgotten
and she could wait to be forgotten

Minerva kept seeing Arachne's weaving
waiting in the daylight
with the daylight passing through it
the weaving reminded Minerva of something
she could not see there
that she could not remember

Arachne's weaving
even where it was broken
was always perfect
with a perfection that Minerva
could not trace nor imitate

her own wisdom laughed at her
and she was angry
what could she do to Arachne
who could weave the gray before daylight

she started the story
about a contest between them
which she won
weaving daylight
and then what could she do
to Arachne to obliterate her
to forget her
as though she had never existed
all day in Minerva's own mind
in her own weaving in her own dream
she could not imagine a way

to unmake Arachne
all night her own bird answered only
Who

the bird knew
she could not change Arachne
into anything but Arachne

in the gray before day
wherever Minerva's gray eyes turned
she saw Arachne's weaving

FOOTHOLDS

Where I dug the logs into the rise
to make the steps along the valley
I forget how many years ago
their wood has dissolved completely now
disappearing into the curled slope
gone without my seeing it happen
while the green clouds of the trees have grown
above their mingled shadows
yet I set my feet down in the same
places I did when the steps were there
without even thinking about them
Father and Mother friend upon friend
what I remember of them now
footholds on the slope
in the silent valley this morning
Wednesday with few clouds and an east wind

BEGINNERS

As though it had always been forbidden to remember
each of us grew up
knowing nothing about the beginning

but in time there came from that forgetting
names representing a truth of their own
and we went on repeating them
until they too began not to be remembered
they became part of the forgetting
later came stories like the days themselves
there seemed to be no end to them
and we told what we could remember of them

though we always forgot where they came from
and forgot that it was forbidden
and whether it had been forbidden
but from forgotten pain we recognize
sometimes the truth when it is told to us
and from forgotten happiness we know
that the day we wake to is our own

OFFERING

Saturday morning and the trades
are back trading out of the east
offering their samples of cloud
each the only one of its kind
and each of them changing even
as it is offered only once
without a word except the one
sound of hushing to say that this
is all happening in secret
this unrepeatable present
only today for the lucky one

ONE DAY MOTH

The lingering late-afternoon light of autumn
waves long wands through the arches
of fronds that meet over the lane
the bright rays dance in the shadow
and a giant moth like a waving hand
of gray velvet unfolds and dances among them
one moment a dappled brightness
and the next another darkness
surfing the shadows now
this shadow in the curve of the lane
that I have known through these years
the place of parting and of returning

THE COLOR THEY COME TO

I do not have to see
in order to believe
I know that the flame tree is flowering
when I see the petals at my feet
where each of them has come down
in its time to its place
out of where it was waiting
in the sky its birthplace
to lie on a green leaf
or a worn stone of the path
each petal alone in the present
curled in its own color

These trees have no names
whatever we call them

where will the meanings be
when the words are forgotten

will I see again
where you are

will you be sitting
in Fran's living room

will the dream come back
will I know where I am

will there be birds

HIGH FRONDS

After sundown the crowns
of the tallest palms
stand out against
the clear glass of the eastern sky
they have no shadows
and no memory
the wind has gone its own way
nothing is missing

GARDEN NOTES

All day in the garden
and at night when I wake to it
at its moment I hear a sound
sometimes little more than a whisper
of something falling
arriving
fallen
a seed in its early age
or a great frond formed
of its high days and nights
looking at the sky
made of daybreak the morning sun
and the whole of daylight
the moon and the stars and the clouds
and of the rain descending out of itself
coming down to its own leaf
there is no trace of regret
in the sound or in the stillness
after the falling
no sound
of hesitation on the way
no question and no doubt

COMING OF AGE

It will not be enough
to recall stills from along the way
to glimpse from its hill
the long-gone night pasture
the light on the river
but not the river
the sunbeam on the scuffed stairs
in the soundless house
but not where it was going
the eyes of a dog
watching from beside me
a face in shadow
silent as an old photograph
our meeting our first night
and waking at home together
again
I was there
these same hands and these eyes as they were
when they wondered where it was going
where it had gone
it will not be enough
it will be enough

A STEP AT A TIME

Now one eye daylight
and one not
there was a lifetime
before they flew
their true colors
but I must have known
the moment I was born
the pans of the balance
swinging along with me
always two poles
with the seasons rocking
between them

and the familiar the unexplored
the city the country
abroad almost at home
and home never quite there
just the way it was before

left foot right foot
on the same way
my own way
of finding and losing
and in my own time
coming to one
love one place
day and night
as they came to me

but the knowing and the rain
the dream and the morning
the wind the pain
the love the burning

it seems you must let them come
so you can let them go
you must let them go
so you let them come

ANOTHER TO *ECHO*

How beautiful you must be
to have been able to lead me
this far with only
the sound of your going away
heard once at a time and then
remembered in silence
when the time was gone
you whom I have never seen
o forever invisible one
whom I have never mistaken
for another voice
nor hesitated to follow
beyond precept and prudence
over seas and deserts
you incomparable one
for whom the waters fall
and the winds search
and the words were made
listening

AMONG THE SHADOWS AT HOME

Life after life at nightfall
in houses I have loved
I see them now here at home
where I walk in shadow
through open doorways
from room to room
leaving the lights off
as I always loved to do
knowing beyond belief
echoes of no sound
from other times other ages
how did I ever find
my way to these rooms now
these shadows
one after the other
through all the loud flashing days
how could I have known
the ancient love of these shadows
with the lights on

THE ETERNAL RETURN

Because it is not here it is eternal
the stars we consider have long been gone
I cannot recall what I was saying
while clouds melted over the morning sea
here is the same child without a childhood
the whole sentence present in the last word
and the morning of what I do not know
brings back everything that I remember
even what is gone and I know it is gone
and know I will never look on it again
appears to me once more almost complete
in its own time and then gone again
it was watching over me while I slept

SUMMER SKY

July with sun-filled leaves drifting among the butterflies
I have been coming to this morning light since the day I was born
I saw its childhood as I sat alone in silence by the high window
no one else saw it no one else would ever recognize it
it is the same child now who watches the clouds change
they appear from out of sight and change as the moment passes
    through them

A BREEZE AT NOON

As I stand at the graves it comes
becoming that moment we have
together that single breath
from beyond Andromeda
from a time before time
it is here at home where I cherish
the flying days and it stirs
the dry leaves of the breadfruit tree
and drops a dead *Pinanga* frond
like an arrow at my feet
and I look up into the green
cluster of stems and gold strings
beaded with bloodred seeds
each of them holding tomorrow
and when I look
the breeze has gone

THE NEW SONG

For some time I thought there was time
and that there would always be time
for what I had a mind to do
and what I could imagine
going back to and finding it
as I had found it the first time
but by this time I do not know
what I thought when I thought back then

there is no time yet it grows less
there is the sound of rain at night
arriving unknown in the leaves
once without before or after
then I hear the thrush waking
at daybreak singing the new song

II

THE GREEN FENCE

My poor father
the French would say
meaning he is dead
as the newspaper announced
almost forty years ago

but I find myself now
calling him poor
for other reasons
I believe he was
afraid all his life

he had been the youngest
surviving child the last hope
trying to please
his dour disappointed mother
then talking his way into
one set of high expectations
after another
expectations that he knew
he was not up to
as though he had borrowed
beyond his means
neither his smiles nor
his outbursts of temper
altogether sound

and my mother
with an orphan's uncertainty
feeling that she was a stranger

wanting to do the correct thing
walking to school with us
to keep us out of trouble
in the rough neighborhood
standing with us in the schoolyard
at recess to keep me
from playing rough games
which were the only games
so I made no friends there

and of course I was never allowed
to play in the street
if anyone called me out
to join them
you have a big yard my father said
you can play in there with them
if you ask me first
so I will know who they are
but none of them would come in there

I watched through the picket fence
that my sister and I
had helped to paint green that summer
over the old blistered brown
that I liked better
because of what it remembered

one day Salvatore
the fat Italian boy

who never played in their games
came and stood outside the fence
looking in between pickets
he had nothing to say
I told him I would tell
my father and he could come in
but he shook his head and sat down
on the sidewalk and looked in
and stayed there for a while
at supper I asked my father
about Salvatore coming in
and he thought and said maybe
is he foreign

another time there was May
who was what they called colored
she was the first colored girl I had seen
she did not play with anyone
she came slowly past the fence
and looked in and stopped
I asked her whether
she would like to come in
and she said nothing
holding on to one picket
I was curious to know
whether her color would rub off
and I touched the backs of her fingers
and for a moment we stood there

dear almost friends what happened
to you after that
you wandered on down the street
and disappeared

I have been back
to where the fence used to be
and no one remembers it

ONLY SPARROWS

By the time I came
only the sparrows
were there

the sparrows of morning
did not remember
the evening sparrows

nothing was known
of any sparrows
from other days

other birds lived only in pictures
but I watched for them
listened for them

I listened early
and through each sip
from the chipped cup

I watched the only tree
for a tree sparrow
the tree and I waited

were there still vespers I asked
and did they still have
their own sparrows

was the song sparrow
singing
anywhere at all

the door never forgets
its old longing
to be a bird

the only sparrows I heard
I was told were the ones
other people had brought

the sparrows said one thing
but only to themselves
and each other

over and over they said
here here
yes here

CANCELLATION

The first school I went to
was torn down a year later
but I still know
the way to it
down the avenue and across
and I carry with me the stories
weightless as shadows
of its cold walls
like crumpled tunnels
roughcast to look real
their silent faces
looking past me
I was smaller than anyone else
too young for the games they were playing
I stood watching until the bell rang
at the end of recess
and the echoes thundered
on the iron stairs
of the building named for
a president whose face
was on a black postage stamp
the color of the stones outside
because he had died in office
the next year we were led
to a new redbrick school
named for the inventor of lightbulbs

RELICS

Before I knew words for it
I loved what was obsolete
crumpled at the foot of a closet
lost in the street
left out in the rain
in its wet story
from another age
in a language that was lost
like the holes in socks
I loved the rust with its steering wheel
in midair above the forbidden
chassis and the mouths of tunnels
the eyes of dust
no floor with its pedals
that I was never to touch
because all of it was
dangerous
and the touch of it
would never come off
though I could tell that no one
really believed that
as it stood there behind
the garage that had floated to us
like an ark from the days of horses
and I stood at the corner and listened

THE HEADBOARD

When I was a child
I slept in the old bed
a boat from another time
with a high headboard and a name
it was Margie's bed
with its own history
that I would never be told

before I went to school
a bell stood on the floor
beside the bed
in case I felt sick in the night
and I knew what it was to be punished
without knowing why

but one night the moon woke me
from the sky across the street
and I got out of bed
to look at it
and stood leaning against the headboard
with my head between
the headboard and the cold wall
and its ancient smell of wallpaper
there Margie's headboard
held me pinned to the wall
and would not let me go

I did not want to call
I went on watching the moon
alone

listening to the still night
hearing a faraway streetcar
a cricket somewhere in the dark
while I watched the moonlight
until Margie's headboard let me go
and I climbed back
into the unknown story
taking that sound with me

FERRIES

They have not gone anywhere for some time now
out of the port where the snow is falling
and it goes on falling slowly as though
it were sliding down glass in silence
and keeps falling steadily through the years

so that I cannot read all the letters
now of the names in black on the panels
up on the top decks in front of the paired
wheelhouses one forward one aft
with the wheels still visible inside them
Weehawken Bergen Yonkers a few
remain partly legible through the snow
the rest are anonymous whited out
and spellbound bundled against each other
filling the whole cove on Staten Island
cataracts cancelling the tiered windows

which of them brought me across the river
from the hospital where I had been born
if they brought me by boat and who watched it come in
saw the ramps go down and I heard for the first time
its chains ring as the capstans turned
and in later days we would walk aboard or ashore
and the living deck under us was an old friend
ready to take us where we meant to go
or to bring us home again and again
it would swing us out onto the water
under the gulls' cries on the real river

and which of those hulls carried me home again
when the time came and the day had gone by
it rang its bells then and blew its whistle
and the black greased pilings of the jetties
fell aside to show the churning water
as we set out from their heavy embrace

I thought the ferries then were practicing
something they had always known how to do
I believed they knew where they were going

THE RIVER ONE SUMMER DAY

Now in its own time the great river
is flowing taking the bright sunlight
but it looks as still as another sky
a puff of white from a boat whistle
waits in no sound while the windows flash
on the afternoon ferries and along
whole railroad trains held still as breaths
hypnotized onto strings of barges
and the day-tour steamer glitters without
moving in front of the glittering
silence of the city it keeps passing
like a clock hand and a liner arriving
with its tugs out ahead like dark kites
in no wind carries without a sound
the whole of arrival it is still
there in that changeless river
though my window has long been gone
and the voice in the room behind me
closing up to go home and the whole
of the church on the edge of the cliff
above the harbor and the vessels
asleep in their berths along the shore

BY THE ALLEGHENY

On the far side of the tracks all day long
people are going up and down the ramp
of the viaduct to the bridge across
the railroad tracks those shining rails
that hum to themselves day and night something
about another world and the way to it
and from beyond the viaduct bare roofs stare
without a thought while far behind them
a huge sign blocks out the range of dark hills
with a flashy caricature of the sun
and something for sale while the real sun
slips down behind the hills without comment
and hidden behind the piles of roofs
the river flows out of ancestral silence
while my grandmother sits looking out that way
toward the river and lifts up her eyes she says
unto the hills from whence her help cometh
oh it had been a beautiful place at one time
forests down to the shore and birds on the water
and it was beautiful to me as I first saw it
and as I see it now when no one else
still beholds the apparition as I do

On the green hill with the river beyond it
long ago and my father there
and my grandmother standing in her faded clothes
wrinkled high-laced black shoes in the spring grass
among the few gravestones inside their low fence
by the small white wooden church
the clear panes of its windows
letting the scene through from the windows
on the other side of the empty room
and a view of the trees over there
my grandmother hardly turned her head
staring like a cloud at the empty air
not looking at the green glass gravestone
with the name on it of the man to whom
she had been married and who had been
my father's father she went on saying nothing
her eyes wandering above the trees
that hid the river from where we were
a place where she had stood with him one time
when they were young and the bell kept ringing

THE GLOAMING

The gloaming the gloaming
it was already long ago
when I heard its name the first time
we used to sing of it
and so I asked what it meant
and they shook their heads slowly
eyes reflecting something gone
but I saw it then even so
without knowing how to say it
the high summer past
and the light of that time
under the spreading trees
the hushed day lingering there
after the sun had gone
after the glare and the voices
a time of waiting
hoping to hear

ON A DISTANT SHORE

The night before sailing
from the world I had known
that now seems the ancient
world to me
it was a hot summer night
in the humming city
the small hours the tiny
two-room apartment of a friend
the windows wide open
above the avenue
and behind me three young women
crammed in asleep
as I stood at the window
and then I turned to the room
and in the light from the street
beheld one beautiful
bare breast of a friend's friend
gently rising and falling
as though I were not there
already not there

ALBA

Climbing in the mist I came to a terrace wall
and saw above it a small field of broad beans in flower
their white fragrance was flowing through the first light
of morning there a little way up the mountain
where I had made my way through the olive groves
and under the blossoming boughs of the almonds
above the old hut of the charcoal burner
where suddenly the scent of the bean flowers found me
and as I took the next step I heard
the creak of the harness and the mule's shod hooves
striking stones in the furrow and then the low voice
of the man talking softly praising the mule
as he walked behind through the cloud in his white shirt
along the row and between his own words
he was singing under his breath a few phrases
at a time of the same song singing it
to his mule it seemed as I listened
watching their breaths and not understanding a word

CAN PALAT

By the time I discovered it
there had been no path to it for years

above the last houses in the narrow
side valley they still called the old vineyard

then up over the terrace walls
through the ancient olive and almond trees

along the lap of the towering cliff
until one of the terraces opened out

to overlook the hill with the village
far below and the sea below that

and on the side of the terrace toward
the mountain the remaining walls

of a house that had been there an age before
that had seen the world through the light there

the curved red tiles along the eaves
three layers of them proclaiming importance

were still painted white on the underside
with designs in black from the remote past

the stone arch of the entrance room
was still standing and the broad stones of the floor

were smooth where they could be seen through the rubble
like the clear sky through a flock of clouds

and on the terrace in front of the house
a circle of wall waist-high remained intact

above the old cistern that had been empty
ever since the roof had fallen in

the chamber below had given up echoing
but nearby on the terrace one living

descendant went on reaching out long arms
an ancient pomegranate tree

gnarled and twisted and the dark bark shredded
the rings inside it holding its long story

and the sap still climbing to make
another life as I sat there by the wall

and I was young and I heard sheep bells far off
a breeze in the almonds a voice

with its echo and a girl singing somewhere
and I thought it might be enough

STILL

Even if I were to return it would not be
the place we came to one evening down a narrow lane
between old walls not far south of Orléans
on the Loiret the clustered village as the sun was sinking
the lane leading down to the edge of the small river
that seemed scarcely to flow between the near shore
and the tangled screen of trees on the far side
a scene Corot would have recognized
with the small child at the water's edge
feeding the ducks that swam over to him
under the gaze of the portly man standing
a few steps behind him thinking about
money and a woman somewhere and dinner
while the seamless water slipped past under the reflections

FORGOTTEN FOUNTAIN

Water dripping year after year
from the green mossed crevice in the east cliff
through my absences and through winter
through the shadows after midday
as they deepened to nightfall
the clear drops arriving through the stone
with no color of their own as they
appear one by one on the threshold
of the world in its full color
and each one pauses for a moment
before starting on its way down
to itself as it has been doing
ever since the cliff rose
from the seafloor and then the bees found it
the badgers the foxes the birds
until the day came with voices
from the village to clear the slope
singing as the tools rose and fell
turning the stiff yellow soil to plant
vineyards and peaches and I stood
by the clear source once listening
to their last singing together
with the mattocks keeping time and I
thought of Édouard and the village
as it had been when he was young
and his name was called with the others
to the colors as they put it
in the language of elsewhere and of

what it felt like in those last days
to be leaving for Verdun with no words
in a moment with no color of its own

THRESHING TIME

Though it has all gone into the palace
and the soundless doors have closed after it
and the whole palace vanished like a cloud
with everyone else who was there that day
standing in a ring beyond the old wall
of the vegetable garden in front
of the empty house where an old woman
had lived before any of them knew her
there they all stood that late-summer day
as I walked back down into the village
from the upland and rounded the corner
I heard their voices the timeless echoes
as their arms rose in turn swinging the flails
in the bronze cloud of light and behind them
hands I knew raised the winnowing baskets
to the breeze at the far end of the house
the sounds floated in silence even then
their hands rose in time through their own distance
threshing for the last time in the old way

AFTER THE VOICES

Youth is gone from the place where I was young
even the language that I heard here once
its cadences that went on echoing
a youth forgotten and the great singing
of the beginning have fallen silent
with the voices that were the spirit of them
and their absences were no more noticed
than were those of the unreturning birds
each spring until there were no words at all
for what was gone but it was always so
I have no way of telling what I miss
I am only the one who misses it

Small roads written in sleep in the foothills
how long ago and I believed you were lost
as I saw the bronze deepening in the light
and the shy moss turning to itself holding
its own brightness above the badger's path
while a single crow sailed west without a sound
and yet we trust without giving it a thought
that we will always see it as we see it once
and that what we know is only
a moment of what is ours and will
always be ours we believe it as
the moment flows away out of reach
and lengthening shadows merge in the valley
and one window kindles there like a first star
what we see again will come to us in secret
and without even knowing that we are here

OLD BREADHOUSE

Here they came when another week had gone
bearing their waving armloads of brambles
dried seasons of their own lives snapping
a last few sharp syllables as the arms
bundled them into the black sunrise
of the oven door to the sound of their own
words that were leaves of an ancient language
they would be the last to speak and they
set the brush ablaze in the brick vault
when the risen loaves were ready to be passed
into place one by one on the long paddles
each loaf as round as an embrace
or as a week or the sky that morning

RUNNING IN THE DARK

A bad dream like a lantern somewhere
ahead of me was casting a beam like a magnet
and I was running toward it across the dark pasture
as I could never have done in the daylight
I kept feeling the breath of that summons
that I thought had been left behind in a destroyed age
I ran untouched past the tangled thornbushes through the
last moments before I learned
what it was that had called me out to it
on the railroad tracks beyond the pasture wall
the mangled floundering bodies of mauled sheep
bleating and coughing dying in the dark
far from where they had been meant to die

THE BELL OF ONE MORNING

The blackbird came in the dark
in the shadow before the first light
of a cold June
thin rain falling a few drops at a time
like friends needing no words
arriving among the infant leaves
of the walnut tree
like small fingers in sleep
after sunrise the bell
did not know why it was ringing
it was for the old schoolteacher
who had fallen silent in the dark

ELEGY FOR A WALNUT TREE

Old friend now there is no one alive
who remembers when you were young
it was high summer when I first saw you
in the blaze of day most of my life ago
with the dry grass whispering in your shade
and already you had lived through wars
and echoes of wars around your silence
through days of parting and seasons of absence
with the house emptying as the years went their way
until it was home to bats and swallows
and still when spring climbed toward summer
you opened once more the curled sleeping fingers
of newborn leaves as though nothing had happened
you and the seasons spoke the same language
and all these years I have looked through your limbs
to the river below and the roofs and the night
and you were the way I saw the world

CLEAR SOUND

Cold spring morning remembering
fewer birds now but their songs ring out
through the mist and the young leaves
that have never seen anywhere else
the songs rise out of themselves knowing the way
no words for before and after
and the singers nowhere to be seen

GARDEN MUSIC

In the garden house
the digging fork and the spade
hanging side by side on their nails
play a few notes I remember
that echo many years
as the breeze comes in with me
out of the summer light
they know the notes by now
so well that the music
seems to be going on
all by itself in the shade
of the roof I made for them
half my life ago
and I see the garden now
far away in itself
reflected in the polished spade
as a place I have never been
while the music goes on
echoing the days

TIME IN THE GRASS

In a few fields the first hay is lying
naked in its new fragrance as its color fades
and no one has stayed to see the noon light
dappling the small growth in the shade of the trees
beside the meadows that are still untouched
where the spring grasses go on rippling
in the shimmering daylight of their lives
and the voles clad in velvet shadows
trickle through their feet under the whispers
of the tall world while the clear notes
of crickets on all sides call keep calling
to the world to stay just as it is
they go on calling even when the grass has gone

Ghosts of words
circle the empty room
where I was young
stars in daylight

not a sound from them
not one question
they know me
in their unseen galaxy
they are my own

the walls that were
whitewashed when they were younger
have turned into
maps of absence

my dog three years gone
and more
oh more
barks in a dream
beside my left hand
watchful as ever
waking me
from that dream

where is she

where am I

OLD PLUM TREE

How long were you there
before I remembered you
as the birds did each year

when I saw you
you were already old

one of your limbs has gone
the twisted trunk is hollow
clasping the dark
some years there were nests
among the branches

you never grew tall
in the thin rocky soil
at the top of the shallow field
common blue plum
what they called pig plum –
after Saint Anthony's pig
so they say
as they feed your delicious
bounty to the pigs
what do you care

in late summer we ate our fill
of your ripe fruit
with the fine velvet still on it
in the July noon
and through the days of August

and we have baked the plums into tarts
and preserved them in jars
for later
and picked up every last
soft fallen fruit out of the grass
in September
to distill the clear spirit
called water of life

who am I to remember
leaves you have forgotten
the flutter of wings

and bird voices there
and your rough bark in each season
and the fragrance of your dry
branches burning

now one more time
your flowers have fallen like a fine snow
and among your new leaves a few
infant green plums the size of raindrops
have appeared

o silent Ancient
age of the daylight

URTICOPHILIA

Oh let me wake where nettles are growing
in the cool first light of a spring morning
the young leaves shining after a night's rain
a green radiance glistening through them
as their roots rise into their day's color
a hue of sunlight out of the black earth
that they made with their roots in the underworld
touching the darkness of their whole story
from which their leaves open to this morning
finding a world they know and a season
they inherit let me wake where nettles
were always familiar and come and go
in the conversation their growth this year
compared with other years in the same places
the way they sting if barely brushed but not
if grasped firmly without hesitation
the best recipe for nettle soup using
new potatoes oh let the world's sense
come to me from the spring leaves of nettles
my true elders and not from the voices
with something to sell nor from the spreading
scar tissue of pavement numbing the flayed earth
not from the latest words of the fast-talkers
to whom the nettle leaves never listen

NEITHER HERE NOR THERE

An airport is nowhere
which is not something
generally noticed

yet some unnamed person in the past
deliberately planned it

and you have spent time there
again
for something you have done
which you do not entirely remember
like the souls in Purgatory

you sit there in the smell
of what passes for food
breathing what is called air
while the timepieces measure
their agreement

you believe in it
while you are there
because you are there
sometimes you may even feel happy
to be that far on your way
to somewhere

THE PALACES

A flight across the clear day of autumn
unheard and unseen by the fair earth far below
deserts broad valleys gorges hung with shadows
faded farmlands with no horizons
blurring far away into gray distances
mountains with darkness flowing out of them
while the passengers were reading or sleeping
or gazing into lighted screens

a voice with no face interrupts to warn us
of thunderstorms as we approach the capital
and of delays at the terminal
and as we begin our descent
we start to bank and circle
with the green growing brighter below us
in the long afternoon light
while the passengers complain
about missed appointments
or they sit white-knuckled as we drop
through a pocket and then through others
beside a looming crag of cloud
lit by gold beams of sinking sunlight

Roy Fuller saw Shakespeare
in the coil of a cloud
Blake's paintings are colored with cloud light
Octavio Paz in his last days
when asked how he was replied
much of the time now I
am in the clouds

but there are wonderful things in the clouds
but he had no words for them

we went on circling and dropping through
sudden shadows beside gray cliffs
icebergs in other lives
we passed through them and around them
back into the whole sunset

the clouds have no names
they answer to no one
they are never late

who saw them
and remembered them
when we had sailed down through them all the way
and the clouds let us go

late

ANCIENT WORLD

Orange sunset
in the deep shell of summer
a long silence reaching
across the dry pastures
in the distance a dog barks
at the sound of a door closing
and at once I am older

RULE OF THUMB

When my thumb touches my little finger
a door opens that I forgot was there
a door of air forgotten in the air

the thumb knows that door through which I came
but what the thumb knows is before knowledge

it does not listen with its map of hearing
it hears the harmony the fingers play

I cannot go back through that door again
and the thumb will not guide me anywhere
pointing the way home for the thumb is there

ONE SUMMER

It is hard now to believe that we really
went back that time years ago to the small town
a mile square along the beach and a little more
than a century old where I had been taken
when I was a child and nothing seemed to have changed
not the porches along the quiet streets
nor the faces on the rockers nor the sea smell
from the boardwalk at the end of the block
nor the smells from the cafeteria in a house
like the others along the same sidewalk
nor the hush of the pebbled streets without
cars nor the names of the same few hotels
nor the immense clapboard auditorium
to which my mother had taken me
to a performance of *Aida*
and you and I walked those streets in a late
youth of our own and along the boardwalk
toward music we heard from the old carousel

CHOOSING

Was it home or foreign
that city without color
where I once lived for a time
that often seemed long
thinking there was no choice
and all night I heard captive lions roaring

now I look back
from when the rain is falling
in the bright day

a friend and I
talked back then about a tree
whose branches were the choices that we
had not taken
then she chose not to be

never was there any such tree

better
the sound of the rain
better the brightness falling
better the day
choosing to be morning

THE LATEST THING

In the cities the birds are forgotten
among other things but then one could say
that the cities are made of absences
of what disappeared so they could be there
the flycatchers after the Algonquins
the slaves and the buildings they had made
the woods and the wood thrushes taking their
songs with them when they went and the leaves
taking the tongues they spoke until one could say
that in the continuous sound of the city
one white note plays on to prevent memory
even of the city itself as it was
yesterday in that very place or just
before the light changed at the street corner
it may be that the sound of a city
is the current music of vanishing
naturally forgetting its own song

WHITE ON WHITE

Above the terraces almost at the top
of the Tower of Babel my eyes are
travelling among the sailing clouds
once more they find themselves at home among
migrating flocks of birds both those that still
return to earth and those that have left it
lying in its losses they fly knowing
their unknowable way and my ears follow them
as they always did toward sounds from before
there was hearing and they ride echoes
into a music more familiar than
I could ever have believed possible
its passions swelling as deep as ever
ringing upward from the bells of the streams
every moment that I loved and had lost
rising toward me to be recognized
the sound of it in the rush of the night rain
I am awake and have been at home the whole time

III

ABOVE THE PURPLE GORGE

As the dream of summer is almost gone
I wake to a beloved dream of autumn
the love of my life is with me and one old woman friend
in the distance the craggy peaks glow like brass
beyond the purple gorge that winds below us
we walk where the black grapes of the harvest
are hanging from trellises older than any of us
in the long sunlight and the goodness of time
and I have come back to hear the mountain songs
sung by the old voices that have kept them
under their breaths in darkness and silence
longer than they are able to tell
their gnarled fingers that pruned the vines
when the last spring snow still glinted in the sunlight
now pluck the strings of the scuffed instruments
modelled upon echoes out of the gorge
which wake once more in the ancient songs
no spring summer or winter ever heard
songs of the stars from before age was born
songs that come back to themselves in the old voices

Mr Daley could whistle between his teeth
but just the one phrase over and over
it was *in the good old summertime*
and it made my mother sniff and shake her head
as he pushed the big wooden spoon around
and around the pot of flour paste he was mixing
on the old coal range in the back kitchen
near the laundry tubs that smelled of laundry tubs
as the flour paste smelled of flour paste
and Mr Daley smelled of Mr Daley
in a stale shirt he was old in his fifties
with a hump between his shoulders and it was
still summertime and he would carry the pot
up the back stairs to the heat of the attic
where he had already carried the truckload
of mattress cartons one at a time
got for nothing from the Furniture Store
& Funeral Parlor on South Main Street
and he had nailed them up under the attic beams
and then would paper them end to end with old
church bulletins as insulation
because the house was so cold in winter
he kept laughing to himself about something
while he worked and whistled they said he was not
like his daughter Isabel whom they admired
who worked in Thomas's Piano Store
that would burn down one winter with icicles
forming from the jets of the fire hoses
and the flames racing up inside the rooms until

the top floors stacked high with pianos
crashed slowly together through icicles
and piano chords chiming in chorus
while I stood watching from across the street
on the stone steps of the Methodist church
remembering Mr Daley whistling
between his teeth in the good old summertime

WEINRICH'S HAND

The wind lifts the whole branch of the poplar
carries it up and out and holds it there
while each leaf is the whole tree reaching
from its roots in the dark earth out through all
its rings of memory to where it has
never been he holds in his fingertips
the moment just before the beginning

that was the stillness he was holding toward
the choir as the chords of the great chorale
gathered rising to its consummation
he was holding between his fingertips
the poplar leaf and the life of the tree
the green of its summer and its seedtime
and chords he had heard before he was born
the organ echoes of his mother's heart

the notes of the cloud chorale rose calling
to each other and he held them as one
held them out to the waiting chorus
then with a quick stroke he cut them off
and silence fell out of the sky like rain

ANTIQUE SOUND

There was an age when you played records
with ordinary steel needles which grew blunt
and damaged the grooves or with more expensive
stylus tips said to be tungsten or diamond
which wore down the records and the music receded
but a friend and I had it on persuasive authority
that the best thing was a dry thorn of the right kind
and I knew where to find those off to the left
of the Kingston Pike in the shallow swale
that once had been forest and had grown back
into a scrubby wilderness alive with
an earthly choir of crickets blackbirds finches
crows jays the breathing of voles raccoons
rabbits foxes the breeze in the thickets
the thornbushes humming a high polyphony
all long gone since to improvement but while
that fine dissonance was in tune we rode out
on bicycles to break off dry thorn branches
picking the thorns and we took back the harvest
and listened to Beethoven's Rassoumoffsky
quartets echoed from the end of a thorn

TELEPHONE RINGING

Telephone Ringing in the Labyrinth
ADRIENNE RICH (1929–2012)

It is you it is you it can only
be you calling and I cannot answer
in time whatever time is with no answer
though I can hear your voice without its words
your own voice yours alone speaking to me
through the dark echoless ageless corridors
of six decades out of reach and beyond
answering if I knew what to answer
then we laughed as we talked about likeness
and difference and the echoes of change
about recognition and its one sound
while we changed without knowing we were
answering but the question was still there
we never answered it I remember now
as I do not answer while it keeps ringing
while it rings on and I do not answer
and still do not know what the question is

THE ARTISAN WORLD

It turns but does not try to remember
it does not precede or follow
obey nor disobey
it is not answering a question
it arrives knowing without knowledge
it makes the pieces one by one in the dark
there is always enough dark
before time comes with the locusts
the insects of comparison the improvers
with their many legs in the dazzling air
makers of multiplication and series
they never touch what is awake here
and is not waiting nor asking nor fashioned
but is one with the uneven current of breathing
with the silence untouched by the rush of noise

WILD OATS

Watching the first sunlight
touch the tops of the palms
what could I ask

All the beads have gone
from the old string
and the string does not miss them

The daughters of memory
never pronounce
their own names

In the language of heaven
the angel said
go make your own garden

I dream I am here
in the morning
and the dream is its own time

Looking into the old well
I see my own face
then another behind it

There I am
morning clouds
in the east wind

No one is in the garden
the autumn daisies
have the day to themselves

All night in the dark valley
the sound of rain arriving
from another time

September when the wind
drops and to us it seems
that the days are waiting

I needed my mistakes
in their own order
to get me here

Here is the full moon
bringing us
silence

I call that singing bird my friend
though I know nothing else about him
and he does not know I exist

What is it that I keep forgetting
now I have lost it again
right here

I have to keep telling myself
why I am going away again
I do not seem to listen

In my youth I believed in somewhere else
I put faith in travel
now I am becoming my own tree

HOW IT HAPPENS

The sky said I am watching
to see what you
can make out of nothing
I was looking up and I said
I thought you
were supposed to be doing that
the sky said Many
are clinging to that
I am giving you a chance
I was looking up and I said
I am the only chance I have
then the sky did not answer
and here we are
with our names for the days
the vast days that do not listen to us

THE WONDER OF THE IMPERFECT

Nothing that I do is finished
so I keep returning to it
lured by the notion that I long
to see the whole of it at last
completed and estranged from me

but no the unfinished is what
I return to as it leads me on
I am made whole by what has just
escaped me as it always does
I am made of incompleteness
the words are not there in words

oh gossamer gossamer breath
moment daylight life untouchable
by no name with no beginning

what do we think we recognize

CONVENIENCE

We were not made in its image
but from the beginning we believed in it
not for the pure appeasement of hunger
but for its availability
it could command our devotion
beyond question and without our consent
and by whatever name we have called it
in its name love has been set aside
unmeasured time has been devoted to it
forests have been erased and rivers poisoned
and truth has been relegated for it
wars have been sanctified by it
we believe that we have a right to it
even though it belongs to no one
we carry a way back to it everywhere
we are sure that it is saving something
we consider it our personal savior
all we have to pay for it is ourselves

DUO AS THE LIGHT IOS GOING

Those two go on with what they are saying
at the ends of their long
lengthening shadows
while the sun sinks in silence
the one gesturing is Painted On
boasting even in silhouette
to Burned In who in response
says not a thing

NATURAL HISTORY OF FORGETTING

When I was me I remembered

I could remember what was not there
but may have been there
once
I could still see where
it had been or they had been
even when no one else
said they remembered

I could remember the man
in the brown suit
who held me up at the front window
the way my mother did
oh that was Aden
my mother said a long time later
I never saw him again
the window has not been there
longer than I can remember
and then there was only her voice
saying that name

when I was me I could not put it in words
though I could hear words waiting
for me to recognize them
ghosts of the unborn
but words could not say it

you remember Tags my father said
pointing to the spot out back

where Tags had been tied
before he was given away
to where he was happy
my father said I remembered him
and so I did
and so I do though I never saw him

when I was me I walked
all over New York
alone and together
together and alone
and where I was going
where we were going and when
I will not know again

when I was me the birds
one by one went away
and did not come back again
and there was no mention
of their presence or their absence

gone beyond going

when I was me
I did not get older
I saw the one measureless
age of clarity
without horizons or beginning
until I began to wake into mist
that became clouds

the beautiful unknowable
once-only clouds
that have no memory

once when I was me
by a clear stream winding
under bushes in a meadow
in the middle of a life
when no one could have known that
I listened to the voices of friends
of many years
along the flowing stream
where we were quietly fishing
for crayfish
once in a single summer

when I was me I forgot

UNKNOWN SOLDIER

Facing us under the helmet
a moment before he is killed
he is a child with a question

LEAR'S WIFE

If he had ever asked me
I could have told him

if he had listened to me
it would have been
another story

I knew them before
they were born

with Goneril at my breast
I looked at the world
and saw blood in darkness
and tried to wake

with Regan at my breast
I looked at the world
and covered my mouth

with Cordelia in my arms
at my breast
I wanted to call out to her
in love and helplessness
and I wept

as for him
he had forgotten me
even before they did

only Cordelia
did not forget
anything
but when asked she said
nothing

IV

IDENTITY

When Hans Hoffmann became a hedgehog
somewhere in a Germany that has
vanished with its forests and hedgerows
Shakespeare would have been a young actor
starting out in a country that was
only a word to Hans who had learned
from those who had painted animals
only from hearing tales about them
without ever setting eyes on them
or from corpses with the lingering
light mute and deathly still forever
held fast in the fur or the feathers
hanging or lying on a table
and he had learned from others who had
arranged the corpses of animals
as though they were still alive in full
flight or on their way but this hedgehog
was there in the same life as his own
looking around at him with his brush
of camel hair and his stretched parchment
of sheepskin as he turned to each sharp
particular quill and every black
whisker on the long twitching snout and those
flat clawed feet made only for trundling
and for feeling along the dark undersides
of stones and as Hans took them in he
turned into the Hans that we would see

THE HERON TIME

That last summer before I was thirty
in the swaybacked old house leaning together
to hold itself up along the Bagaduce
chipmunks in the ceiling of every room
the smell of their nests a kind of company
I would get up before daybreak and slip out
trying not to wake the red squirrel
but always failing and he screamed
Bad Man Bad Man to the whole world
from a branch right over me
until I came to the edge of a clear-cut
and crossed it in the silence of a clear-cut
to the forest of towering firs
with the river mist sifting through their crowns
and the loud water
half hidden below them
under its cold white shawl
I moved quietly hoping to get close
to the river birds wading near the bank
and in the river roar I came
to the great blue heron standing
just in front of me
motionless for a moment
I could not measure
then his wings opened
and without moving them he was gone

CLOP CLOP

In my hand a small
iron arc
old and worn
long ago
with five empty holes
for square nails

clop clop

the good carts
survive the donkeys
their shafts in the air
the polished plows
outlast the last horses
then slowly they turn back
to the color of earth
clop clop

I hear
the cuckoo
too
far in another
season
another year
this season
this year

even on the new road

clop clop

VOICE OF SUMMER

When I hear the cuckoo
it is my own bird
again
that I have not heard
for I forget how long
the bird I have seldom seen
whose call I never forget

cu – cuckoo
it calls again
in its summer
and from the summer of memory
but in the moment when it calls
there is no memory

only the hush of the pasture
with the sheep in the evening
all the years at once
in the lengthening shadows
between the oaks along the ridge
and the broad valley glittering far below

who heard it
just now

who remembers

where is it now
listening
beyond the sheep grazing
in the long shadows

A BLACK KITE

These long cool days at the end of spring
begin with a soundless blaze at sunrise
above the distant rim of the valley
all day clouds gather and clear again
as I remember other cold springtimes here
through the coming and going of years
the losses the changes the long love come to at last
with the river down there flowing through it all
under the clear moment that never changed
in all that time not asking for anything
still the wren sings and the oriole remembers
and every evening now a black kite
glides low overhead coming from the upland
alone not climbing the thermals not hunting
not calling not busy about anything
wings and tail scarcely moving as he
slips out above the open valley
filled with the long gold light before sunset
sailing into it only to be there

FOX FIRE

Remember me
but you cannot remember me

you cannot
remember the first time you saw me
how did you know
me then

how
if you had never
seen me before

where did you think
the light was coming from
the small cloud glowing
dancing slowly
god of the glowworms
above the dark oaks
there in the hollow
behind the hill

behind the rough monument
to a day you had not seen there
never forget it said

at times I watched you
through the daylight
from closer than you
would have believed

I was the moment before
I was the blank in your memory
I was the one thing
you had just forgotten

you never heard me
to you I had no voice
no one else heard me either
but when you saw me you listened
when you watched for me
you listened

you with your many questions
I have none

you ask where I go
even when you see me

you with your names for me
from other voices
times places
serious names saints' names
mocking names childish names
will-o'-the-wisp I have
no name

no country
and I come to you where I please
seen or unnoticed
wherever you may be

and I have no answer
but you never forget me
whether you know it or not

I have no age
you do not have to
believe in me
living or dead

I like long evenings
in spring in autumn
mist is a friend
I am alien
to expectations
absent from definitions

I am not to be lured
not to be caught
like a poor fish

I was the light when the board creaked
just then
I am not to be called back

when you saw me
I was never
anyone else

TURNING

Going too fast for myself I missed
more than I think I can remember

almost everything it seems sometimes
and yet there are chances that come back

that I did not notice when they stood
where I could have reached out and touched them

this morning the black Belgian shepherd dog
still young looking up and saying

Are you ready this time

THE CHAIN TO HER LEG

If we forget Topsy
Topsy remembers

when we forget her mother
gunned down in the forest
and forget who killed her
and to whom they sold
the tusks the feet the good parts
and how they died and where
and what became of their children
and what happened to the forest
Topsy remembers

when we forget how
the wires were fastened on her
for the experiment
the first time
and how she smoldered and
shuddered there
with them all watching
but did not die
when we forget
the lit cigarette
the last laugh gave her
lit end first
as though it were a peanut
the joke for which she
killed him
we will not see home again

when we forget the circus
the tickets to see her die
in the name of progress
and Edison and the electric chair
the mushroom cloud will go up
over the desert
where the west was won
the *Enola Gay* will take off
after the chaplain's blessing
the smoke from the Black Mesa's
power plants will be
visible from the moon
the forests will be gone
the extinctions will accelerate
the polar bears will float
farther and farther away
and off the edge of the world
that Topsy remembers

NO FLAG

After he set up the flag
at the pole where no one ever
had been before him and after
his return and the fanfares
the flags the speeches the medals
the fame he had dreamed about
the praise of kings he came
to the unmapped cold of death
and passed backward through clouds
of speeches that had no sound
and back through curtains of flags
without motion or color stacked
like layered shadows around him
a lifetime of dark draperies
where nothing was known they too
were gone and he saw only
white space under cloud and through it
the ice of his own eyes
and beyond that ice he beheld
in a row watching him
the dogs that had drawn his sled
and brought his whole expedition
to the invisible pole
and had watched him set up the flag
and call out to no one
in a strange voice there they all were
the dogs that he had killed then
and eaten and fed to those
that would take him back again
they went on watching him
where no one had ever been

A MESSAGE TO PO CHU-I

In that tenth winter of your exile
the cold never letting go of you
and your hunger aching inside you
day and night while you heard the voices
out of the starving mouths around you
old ones and infants and animals
those curtains of bones swaying on stilts
and you heard the faint cries of the birds
searching in the frozen mud for something
to swallow and you watched the migrants
trapped in the cold the great geese growing
weaker by the day until their wings
could barely lift them above the ground
so that a gang of boys could catch one
in a net and drag him to market
to be cooked and it was then that you
saw him in his own exile and you
paid for him and kept him until he
could fly again and you let him go
but then where could he go in the world
of your time with its wars everywhere
and the soldiers hungry the fires lit
the knives out twelve hundred years ago

I have been wanting to let you know
the goose is well he is here with me
you would recognize the old migrant
he has been with me for a long time
and is in no hurry to leave here
the wars are bigger now than ever

greed has reached numbers that you would not
believe and I will not tell you what
is done to geese before they kill them
now we are melting the very poles
of the earth but I have never known
where he would go after he leaves me

VARIATION ON A THEME

Thank you my lifelong afternoon
late in this season of no age
thank you for my windows above the rivers
thank you for the true love you brought me to
when it was time at last and for words
that come out of silence and take me by surprise
and have carried me through the clear day
without once turning to look at me
thank you for friends and long echoes of them
and for those mistakes that were only mine
for the homesickness that guides the young plovers
from somewhere they loved before
they woke into it to another place
they loved before they ever saw it
thank you whole body and hand and eye
thank you for sights and moments known
only to me who will not see them again
except in my mind's eye where they have not changed
thank you for showing me the morning stars
and for the dogs who are guiding me

THE PROW OF THE ARK

What I remember I cannot tell
though it is there in all that I say
the scrape of the prow on the mountain
after the forty dark days of rain
and the boundless flood of forgetting
drifting without a sail or rudder
with the bedlam of the animals
lost calls roars whistles shrieks and never
an answer and then the sound of wings
as he released the raven and as
it flew away never to return
days later the dove's wings bringing back
the olive twig out of the daylight
then in one first gray before daybreak
the sound of the mountain holding them
hushed above the tide of forgetting
and the doors finally shrieked open
and one by one the animals came
out into the round glare of silence
and by daylight their shadows found them
then female and male they went in pairs
away again into the first time
and the shipwright and his family
took their words and tools and their first steps
on the earth and were all forgotten
it was soon impossible to say
whether the name for him was his real name
or whether he had ever existed
though we have heard the scrape of the prow

W.S. Merwin has published more than twenty books of poetry, including *The Shadow of Sirius*, which won the 2009 Pulitzer Prize; *Present Company*; *Migration: New & Selected Poems*, which won the 2005 National Book Award; *The Pupil*; *The River Sound*, which was named a *New York Times* Notable Book of the Year; *Flower and Hand: Poems 1977–1983*; *The Vixen*; and *Travels*, which received the Lenore Marshall Poetry Prize.

He has also published over twenty books of translation, including *Sir Gawain & the Green Knight*; Dante's *Purgatorio*; and volumes by Yosa Buson, Musō Soseki, Pablo Neruda, Federico García Lorca, and more.

Merwin was most recently named the first Laureate of the Zbigniew Herbert International Literary Award. His other honors include the Lannan Literary Award for Lifetime Achievement, the Aiken Taylor Award for Modern American Poetry, the Bollingen Prize, a Ford Foundation grant, the Governor's Award for Literature of the State of Hawaii, the Ruth Lilly Poetry Prize, the PEN Translation Prize, the Shelley Memorial Award, the Wallace Stevens Award, and a Lila Wallace–Reader's Digest Writers' Award, as well as fellowships from the Academy of American Poets, the Guggenheim Foundation, the National Endowment for the Arts, and the Rockefeller Foundation.

He is a former Chancellor of the Academy of American Poets and has served as Poetry Consultant to the Library of Congress. In 2010, Merwin was appointed the Library of Congress's seventeenth Poet Laureate Consultant in Poetry. He currently lives and works in Hawaii.

Copper Canyon Press is grateful to the following individuals whose extraordinary financial support made publication of this book by W.S. Merwin possible.

John Branch
David G. Brewster and Mary Kay Sneeringer
Diana and Jay Broze
Maureen Lee and Mark Busto
Sarah and Tim Cavanaugh
Janet and Les Cox
Mimi Gardner Gates
Mark Hamilton and Suzie Rapp
Jeanne Marie and Rhoady Lee
Brice Marden
Penny and Jerry Peabody
Joseph C. Roberts
William and Ruth True
Cynthia Lovelace Sears and Frank Buxton
Charles and Barbara Wright

Poetry is vital to language and living. Since 1972, Copper Canyon Press has published extraordinary poetry from around the world to engage the imaginations and intellects of readers, writers, booksellers, librarians, teachers, students, and donors.

WE ARE GRATEFUL FOR THE MAJOR SUPPORT PROVIDED BY:

THE PAUL G. ALLEN
FAMILY FOUNDATION

the
P●INT
WHERE LESS IS MORE

golden
lasso

Lannan

THE MAURER FAMILY
FOUNDATION

NATIONAL
ENDOWMENT
FOR THE ARTS

WASHINGTON STATE
ARTS COMMISSION

Anonymous
Arcadia Fund
John Branch
Diana and Jay Broze
Beroz Ferrell & The Point, LLC
Janet and Les Cox
Mimi Gardner Gates
Gull Industries, Inc.
on behalf of William and Ruth True
Mark Hamilton and Suzie Rapp
Carolyn and Robert Hedin
Steven Myron Holl
Lakeside Industries, Inc.
on behalf of Jeanne Marie Lee
Maureen Lee and Mark Busto
Brice Marden
New Mexico Community Foundation
H. Stewart Parker
Penny and Jerry Peabody
Joseph C. Roberts
Cynthia Lovelace Sears and Frank Buxton
The Seattle Foundation
Dan Waggoner
Charles and Barbara Wright
The dedicated interns and faithful
volunteers of Copper Canyon Press

To learn more about underwriting Copper Canyon Press titles,
please call 360-385-4925 ext. 103

The Chinese character for poetry is made up of two parts: "word" and "temple." It also serves as pressmark for Copper Canyon Press.

This book is set in MVB Verdigris, a digital typeface by Mark van Bronkhorst, inspired by Jean Jannon and Pierre Haultin's metal types cut in sixteenth-century France. Display type set in Classica Light, designed by contemporary typographer Thierry Puyfoulhoux. Book design by VJB/Scribe.